SEPTEMBER 11, 2001: A DAY IN HISTORY

To order additional copies of this book, contact:
Xlibris
1-888-795-4274
www.Xlibris.com
Orders@Xlibris.com

ISBN: Softcover   978-1-4134-0497-5
         EBook   978-1-4771-6353-5

Print information available on the last page

Rev. date: 10/07/2019

★ ★ ★

SEPTEMBER 11, 2001: A DAY IN HISTORY

written by EVELYN B. BLOCK
illustrated by LESLIE COURTNEY ADLER

It was a clear, beautiful morning in New York City. The twin towers of the World Trade Center glistened in the bright sunshine.

Many people were going to work or to school, walking or traveling on buses, subways, trains, cars, or ferries. Others were at home, just beginning their day.

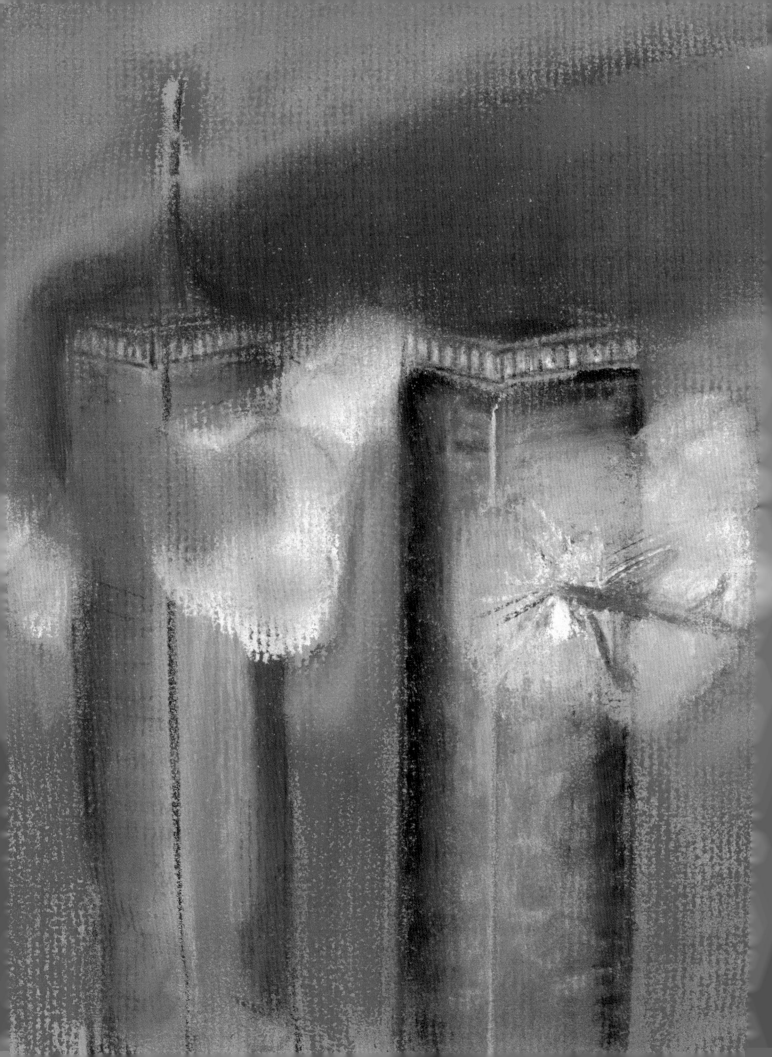

Suddenly, a plane crashed into the north tower of the World Trade Center. A big fire could be seen near the top of the tall building.

Firefighters, police, emergency workers, and others rushed to the building. They wanted to help people escape from the tower and to put out the fire. Each one had a job to do. As employees, visitors to the building, and others rushed down the stairs, they passed firefighters carrying heavy fire fighting equipment up the stairs. They were glad to see that help was arriving.

Eighteen minutes later, a second plane hit the south tower of the World Trade Center. It, too, caught fire. Then another plane hit the Pentagon in Washington, D.C. and a fourth plane crashed in Pennsylvania.

That day, some people walked down 84 flights of stairs to safety. People helped one another as best they could. Some people helped carry others who couldn't walk. Outside, ambulances were waiting to take the injured to the hospital.

People became very frightened as they began to realize that these crashes were not accidents. Something very bad was happening.

The massive explosions and the fires that followed filled the New York skyline with smoke and flames. People were still trying to escape from the two buildings when suddenly, at 10 o'clock in the morning, the south tower of the World Trade Center came crashing to the ground. The north tower fell soon afterwards. Fire engines, ambulances, police cars and other vehicles were crushed by the falling steel and concrete.

Hundreds of people ran as fast as they could to get away from the black smoke, the dreadful noises, the shaking and the falling debris. They ran as fast as they could to safety. Many people were hurt by the smoke and falling objects but were helped by acts of courage from strangers. Some of those strangers later became their good friends.

People tried to call one another to find out if the workers and visitors in the World Trade Center were safe. Those who escaped from the twin towers wanted to tell their families and friends that they were OK. Because the towers had fallen, a lot of telephones and cell phones did not work. Many people were frightened and worried. Citizens all over the world were learning about what had happened in America.

★★★

After the towers finished falling, the area was filled with terrible odors, smoke and dirt. A gray powder covered everything – the pavement, bicycles, benches, signs and fire hydrants. Despite all of the commotion, it became eerily quiet. What had once been a busy, bustling part of New York City was now a huge mass of twisted steel and burning fires. The area came to be known as Ground Zero.

People were overwhelmed, shocked, angry and sad that such a tragedy could happen to our country.

Ground Zero

Everyone soon realized that the four airplanes had been hijacked. It is believed that the brave people on the plane that crashed in Pennsylvania fought with the hijackers to prevent that plane from destroying the Capitol building in Washington, D.C. All the pilots, flight attendants, and passengers on the four hijacked planes died that sad day. Many of them used their cell phones and the telephones on the airplanes to call the people they loved to tell them what was happening. No one on the ground could help them.

President George W. Bush called the attack "a national tragedy." He said, "Two airplanes have crashed into the World Trade Center in an apparent terrorist attack on our country. I have spoken to the vice-president, the governor of New York and the director of the FBI and have ordered that the full resources go to help the victims and their families and to conduct a full-scale investigation to hunt down and find those folks who committed this act. Terrorism against our nation will not stand."

All the airplanes in the sky all over our country had to land at the nearest airport or stay on the ground. The usually busy skies were empty. The electricity went out in parts of New York City and some subway lines were not working, so people used other means of transportation to get home. Many people walked for miles that day. Some took ferries across the river to New Jersey. Help was waiting for them there.

12

On that day, many people wanted to help. As sad and shocked as all Americans felt, people sprang into action. The mayor of New York City, Rudolph Giuliani, immediately rushed to the site to support the rescue and recovery effort. He and George Pataki, the governor of the state of New York, worked tirelessly that day and for many weeks thereafter to lead New York City and to comfort both survivors and victims' relatives and friends. Firefighters, police, emergency workers and volunteers quickly came from all over the New York, New Jersey and Connecticut area to assist the victims and to try to pull survivors from the rubble. Men and women rushed to Red Cross centers to donate blood to help those who had been injured or burned.

Shelters were set up for people who weren't able to return to their homes. Food and blankets were collected for those in need. Doctors, nurses and mental health professionals donated their time to help people cope with the tragedy.

Churches, synagogues, mosques and other houses of worship opened their doors for people who wanted to come together to pray. People who had been working in the twin towers were still missing. Most of them had not survived the attacks. No one could yet know how many people had died that tragic day.

After several days of very exhausting work the heroic rescue effort became a recovery effort. No one else was found alive and the workers turned to the grim task of finding bodies and trying to have them identified. People who were missing were now, sadly, presumed to be dead. Again, a great sadness came upon us. The work continued and the workers grew weary. Families had funerals and memorial services for their lost loved ones. People from all over the world expressed their sympathy about the tragedy that had struck our country.

People all over the United States showed their support for New York and for our country. Everywhere, flags were displayed. People hung flags in front of their homes and displayed them on their cars. Businesses displayed large flags on flagpoles. Giant flags hung from bridges throughout country, including the Golden Gate Bridge in California and the George Washington Bridge, which connects New Jersey and New York.

Americans wanted the world to know that we stood together as a nation. We had been hurt, but we were ready to protect our freedom. The president declared war on those who had committed these attacks, and said we would do whatever it takes to protect the freedom of our country and the freedom of people all over the world.

An evil man named Osama bin Laden and al-Qaida, the terrorist network that he headed, had planned and carried out the attacks against the United States, including the destruction of the twin towers. Osama bin Laden lived in the mountains of Afghanistan. He was being protected by the Taliban, a militant group that had gained control of most of Afghanistan.

When President Bush demanded that the Taliban hand over Osama bin Laden, the Taliban refused. It was then that the United States and its allies launched a military campaign against the Taliban. Soldiers went off to fight in Afghanistan and there were massive air strikes. By the end of 2001, the United States and its allies forced the Taliban from power in Afghanistan but were not able to capture Osama bin Laden. No one knew whether he was still alive or had died. More than six months after the tragic events of September 11, 2001 soldiers from the United States and the new government in Afghanistan continued to try to find Osama bin Laden and to destroy the terrorist network.

In the meantime, the rescue work at Ground Zero continued. Police, firefighters, emergency workers, ironworkers, sheet metal workers, carpenters and drivers of heavy machinery arrived on the scene. Bulldozers, cranes, excavators, power shovels, diggers, backhoes, loaders, and other industrial machines were brought in to help do the hard work. The large melted mess of steel and concrete needed to be pulled apart in an attempt to recover bodies. Many smaller fires were still burning and needed to be extinguished.

★★★

In the end, it took several weeks to put out all the smoldering fires. Men and women worked for hours and hours without a break and soon they were very tired and hungry.

Several dogs became heroes as well, for they were able to go into small places that people couldn't reach and assist in the rescue and recovery effort. Some of the dogs had burned paws and singed hair from their hard work. Doctors, veterinarians and volunteers tended to the dogs and other injured and tired rescue workers.

During this time, people from all over the United States, including from as far away as California, came to help. A large boat docked near the site so tired rescue workers could go on board for a shower and some sleep. The workers were glad to have a place close by to change, shower and rest. Some of them worked 24-hour shifts without stopping. They were determined to remove as much debris as they could, as quickly as they could, in case they could find survivors.

Clothing companies donated shirts, pants, socks and boots so rescue workers could have clean, dry clothing. Families, communities, and restaurants cooked thousands of meals and delivered them to a makeshift kitchen to be reheated and served to the tired workers. Adults and teenagers delivered thousands of bottles of water to thirsty and tired workers. Children sent cards and pictures to encourage the tired workers.

Everyone was sad, yet determined to help in any way that they could. We would show Osama bin Laden that we were not afraid and would protect our freedom.

Everyone worked together to lessen the pain of our great losses. It was briefly a time like the one Martin Luther King and John F. Kennedy and other great statesmen had envisioned: people, regardless of color, creed or nationality, united in the common goals of lending a helping hand where it was needed to ease the suffering and stopping terrorism all over the world.

The cleanup at the World Trade Center continued for many months. Slowly, people who lived in the surrounding area were able to return to their jobs, homes and schools. Streets and subway lines were reopened so people could once again resume their routines. Businesses and restaurants in the area near where the Twin Towers had once stood were thoroughly cleaned and once again open for business.

Americans began to discuss ways to rebuild the area and at the same time create a lasting memorial to the 343 firefighters and almost 3,000 others who had died on September 11, 2001. We worked hard to think of new ways to keep our country safe. We made our airports safer.

On March 11, 2002, in remembrance of the tragedy that had occurred six months earlier, a memorial service was held at Ground Zero. Because it would take a long time to rebuild the buildings and build a permanent memorial at the site, a very special temporary memorial was designed. Two parallel beams of light created by 88 searchlights were turned on each evening at dusk and turned off at 11 o'clock. The two beams of blue light represented the twin towers and were beamed towards the heavens. They remained lit for over a month as planning continued for a more permanent memorial. At the same time, a now badly damaged sphere that had stood in the World Trade Center plaza, between the twin towers, and that had been a symbol of unity and world peace, was installed in Battery Park, near the site of the twin towers.

The damaged sphere and the two beams of light that reached towards the heavens symbolized our loss, our strength, our unity, and our belief in the future of our great nation that was changed forever on September 11, 2001.

Printed in the United States
by Baker & Taylor Publisher Services